PASSION FOR PRIMITIVES

Folk Décor for Interior Design

Franklin & Esther Schmidt

Schiffer Publishing Ltd

4880 Lower Valley Road • Atglen, PA • 19310

Schiffer Books are available at special
discounts for bulk purchases for sales
promotions or premiums. Special editions,
including personalized covers, corporate
imprints, and excerpts can be created in
large quantities for special needs. For more
information contact the publisher:

Published by Schiffer Publishing Ltd.
4880 Lower Valley Road
Atglen, PA 19310
Phone: (610) 593-1777;
Fax: (610) 593-2002
E-mail: Info@schifferbooks.com

For the largest selection of fine reference
books on this and related subjects, please
visit our website at
www.schifferbooks.com
We are always looking for people to write books
on new and related subjects. If you have an idea
for a book, please contact us at
proposals@schifferbooks.com

This book may be purchased from the publisher.
Include $5.00 for shipping.
Please try your bookstore first.
You may write for a free catalog.

In Europe, Schiffer books are distributed by
Bushwood Books
6 Marksbury Ave.
Kew Gardens
Surrey TW9 4JF England
Phone: 44 (0) 20 8392 8585;
Fax: 44 (0) 20 8392 9876
E-mail: info@bushwoodbooks.co.uk
Website: www.bushwoodbooks.co.uk

DEDICATION

This book, as all our work, is dedicated to our eternally supportive parents, Joseph and Emma Schmidt, and Bernard and Marion Godwin, with love.

Jigmop at Dogpatch is always at the heart of things.

CONTENTS

ACKNOWLEDGMENTS

Our gratitude goes to all our editors and art directors at many of the magazines for which we work on so many exciting and challenging projects – with special acknowledgment to Donna Marcel who has led us to a greater understanding of the world of primitives.

We so appreciate the support of our friends in our adopted home, Rappahannock County, Virginia, who have become extended family – as well as our dear friends and relatives across the country, abroad, and even on the high seas.

This book would not have been possible without the generous hospitality and gracious cooperation of hundreds of homeowners throughout the U.S. who have welcomed us into their homes, shared their friendship and that of their dogs and cats and allowed us to photograph their treasured primitives. We have learned so much from them. To paraphrase the sign that hangs in so many country and primitive shops around the country, we came as strangers and left as friends.

Special acknowledgment and thanks to Frances Sip, our friend, associate, and sharer of jelly beans, who helps keep our studio on an even keel.

Thanks are also in order to Schiffer Books and their professional staff, including Pete Schiffer, Douglas Congdon-Martin, and Jesse Marth.

— Franklin & Esther Schmidt

Opposite: Primitive table and small cupboard share simplicity and clean lines.

PRIMITIVES — RUSTIC, IMPERFECT, sensual, historic. Primitive furniture, household artifacts, and two- and three-dimensional folk art — are wildly popular with a wide range of homeowners, interior designers and collectors, from country purists to those who prefer contemporary décor.

The unpretentious honesty of these pieces comes from the imaginations and hearts of untrained artisans, unschooled by traditional educational and apprenticeship processes. These objects evoke immediate and emotional reactions to their beauty. Inspired by internalized concepts of their makers, primitives range from exquisitely simple to embellished.

Primitives were most often created to satisfy a utilitarian need, although some were made, as the Amish say, "just for pretty." They are more about function than form; the art is often serendipitous. By their folk artistry and sculptural presence they have become respected icons of individual design ingenuity.

In this book, readers will see how primitives equate with simple elegance.

They will discover why, always popular with country decorators, primitives are now being incorporated into an even larger arena in the design spectrum. The main focus of the book is to help readers understand and utilize primitives within all aspects of design and décor.

Today's home design says that less is more. Furniture with clean lines and made of natural materials fills furniture markets. We're simplifying our lives and homes. Now, whether a house is antique-based, contemporary in design, or an eclectic mix, primitives have become an even more compelling form for a greater mix of people.

This design trend accounts for the renewed *Passion for Primitives*.

Despite the increasing interest in primitives, there is relatively little in the media that talks specifically about them. As photographers and writers working throughout the U.S., and often in antique and country venues, we hear from designers, homeowners, and decorators who want more and better information about primitives and the best way to incorporate them in interior design.

Even among design and antique experts, there is some confusion and misunderstanding about primitive pieces. Many are drawn to the look but are unsure exactly how it could fit into their décor and home style. *Passion for Primitives* shows and tells the hows and whys of understanding, appreciating, and utilizing primitive furniture.

Passion for Primitives is not a textbook, nor is it encyclopedic and meant to cover every detail of primitive furniture and home design. The emphasis is to show by example. Photography driven, the text and photo captions support the images. Although the book is more "how to" than "history," we include some background text, placing primitives within American design traditions.

What they are and where we found them

IN CREATING THIS BOOK, WE ASKED homeowners, collectors, and antiques dealers throughout the U.S. how they would define a primitive. Most described them as "handmade;" others said that a primitive piece is about a "feeling" — and you just know it by looking at it. One avid collector and expert on the topic simply said "primitives are me." We then asked how they would define primitive as opposed to country, and the best we heard was that primitive pieces are, indeed, country pieces, but country pieces could also be manufactured, whereas primitives are one-of-a-kind and handmade.

That is exactly what we found ourselves searching for in taking, editing, and including the pictures for this book — those pieces that are one-of-a-kind, handmade, and speak of a rural heritage.

Love of primitives knows no region. We found them in homes in the mountains of West Virginia, the plains of Indiana, the small communities of Ohio. They were in living rooms in Arizona and in refurbished antebellum manses near cotton fields in Mississippi; in upscale, trendy lofts in former warehouse districts of Alexandria, Virginia, and suburban homes near Boston. We found primitives — and an appreciation for them — in doublewides in trailer parks and walk-up urban brownstones.

We discovered them in some of the best shops on Madison Avenue as well as flea markets near Louisville. There are websites devoted to them and thousands of bloggers who write about their love of primitives, exchange pictures of their own pieces, and talk about their never-ending search for the next great one.

Looking for some terra firma

TODAY, WE ARE HURTLING THROUGH a world of cyber change. One can access 300 readable books on an electronic tablet no bigger than a hand; individuals communicate instantly with thousands — if not millions — of people around the globe; machinery the size of molecules is commonplace; electronic devices are being designed to read our dreams; food is manufactured more than it is grown. We try to keep up and stretch for handholds as we climb a steepening learning curve. Change has always been part of the human condition, but now it is accelerating beyond our grasp.

Opposite: This is a rare antique sugar chest. This form was used to store sugar shaped into cones. More valuable than cash, especially in the Civil War-torn southern states, sugar was hard to find. Like so many southern pieces, the chest is primarily made of yellow pine, cut thick and then chamfered along the edges so it would appear to be thinner. We can find all the sugar we want, but to find an early primitive sugar chest in mint condition is the rarity.

As a reaction to the dizzying acceleration of life-altering inventions and innovations, society needs to find some solid footing by returning to the firmer ground of things traditional. Restaurants are rediscovering and promoting farm-to-table menu items, trying to hook on to the trendy concept of the simpler (and healthier) life. Once again, farming is in. "Artisan," "handmade," and "homemade" are the new advertising catchwords as we search for a comfort zone. We want clothing made of natural fabrics and foods grown without hormones. A renewed appreciation of the back-to-basics primitive furnishings is in keeping with that.

This is part of the non-verbal definition that lovers and collectors of primitives describe when they attempt to explain their interest in that style. We want to go home again and enjoy the natural, physical world around us — and make it part of our lives. We want to get off the speeding escalators that are taking us away from the familiar.

Primitives reflect the lives and labors of people who are part of the past sinew and strength of our society. Putting this book together has not only enlightened us as to how universally loved — and cherished — this style is, but has also educated us to the many ways that primitive furnishings are incorporated into American homes. We are passing on, through these pages, what we have seen and learned as to how people have enriched their environments with these objects.

While most of the book is dedicated to suggesting design ideas for readers' homes, there are some pictures included in these pages just because the pieces shown are so fabulous we just couldn't resist including them. As another lover of primitives, we know you'll understand.

Opposite: This primitive chest is a prime example of a maker who had probably, at some point, seen some refined furniture and who made the effort to imitate Chippendale-style feet. Or, it could be that once upon a time, the body of the chest was married to the base. Either way, it's a great look and serves a functional purpose.

Opposite Inset: This antique pewter collection is displayed on a deep-toned, milk painted step-back cupboard. The term, step-back refers to the upper portion being more shallow than the bottom, this creating a shelf on the top of the bottom portion of the piece. It's also sometimes referred to as a setback.

CHAPTER I:

FURNITURE...

THE ACCIDENTAL ART

ALL FURNITURE, WHETHER FINELY crafted, highly embellished 18th century Federal, deeply carved 19th century Victorian, or mid-20th century industrially made of aluminum and plastic, has a function. However, none of it was made more with function overriding style than primitives.

Early primitive furniture is basic, simple, imperfect, minimally adorned, usually family made, and one-of-a-kind. It can also be sculptural and artful, but this was rarely its primary intention. The critical element was use. Since most makers lived rurally and had limited resources in time, money and energy, making art was not a high priority. Primitives were primarily created because rural households needed chairs, tables, bucket benches, cupboards, and other practical furnishings. That didn't mean that those country people, who designed and made their own furniture, didn't also have an eye for, and a need to, create something beautiful.

Although many of these pieces were structurally basic, even these most simple furnishings could be elegant in their lines and proportions. Some were even remakes of old, family pieces that had fallen into disrepair. Without any cabinet-making training or experience, somehow their makers innately had — or developed — an instinctive feel for the beauty of the grain of wood; they were intuitively attuned to the surface color that these pieces should be, whether natural or milk painted.

We could be looking at a scene that was one or even two hundred years ago in this attic space. Two great primitives set in low light create a world away from ours.

Opposite: The pine dough box is enhanced by the primitive George Washington portrait. Note the large, exterior, and massively uneven dovetails on the box.

This little, hand carved bucket bench is as one of a kind as it gets – not much is even or symmetrically made in this wonderful piece.

Today, when we assess the quality of those pieces that we either inherit or that have made their way to the market, we are in awe of how well designed and constructed they were. They got hard use and were passed from one generation to the next, but survived through it all.

Still, going beyond the surface assessment, the appeal, appreciation, and understanding of primitive furniture are as much about their makers as the pieces themselves.

Given their likely limited training and experience in furniture making, as well as the lack of availability of fine wood and carving tools, the makers did their best to create furniture that would not only suit a necessary purpose, but would withstand the rugged lifestyle in which it would be utilized. It is even more impressive how often, armed only with an innate feeling for balance, proportion, and surface, they produced pieces that were so artful. Some might call primitives accidental art.

Note the trouble the maker went to in creating the curved apron on the base of this early and elegant cabinet in this primitive-style home in West Virginia.

Opposite: The original red wash on this dry sink makes a very quiet piece stand out.

What it is on the surface

LIKE THEIR MAKERS, MOST PRIMITIVE furniture is direct and simple. Lines are clean; there is little, if any, scrolling and embellishment. The joinery is purposeful; there may be some pegged or mortised joining, but most often pieces are simply butt-joined with nails. Some pieces may be mitered, although there is less of that in the primitive world of furniture. There is no waste of energy, space or material.

The surfaces are unpolished, flat, and opaque and are either milk

The naively-painted scene on the old window adds a great balance to the deeply blue primitive dry sink that also serves as a catch-all cupboard in this kitchen corner on the Arkansas-Mississippi border.

painted, stained, or plain (some call this natural tone or attic finish). A note on milk paint: Although it has been around for thousands of years, people often ascribe milk paint (an amalgam of milk, lime, and natural dyes) to primitive furniture. In today's primitive buying market, most people put a premium on milk painted pieces — and one often hears that "color is king."

Blue, mustard, salmon, and red bring top dollar and have become the premium, pricier surfaces — more so than the also popular, but often less expensive, blacks, whites and browns. However the desirability of most favored colors can tend to be trendy and experienced collectors focus on the overall look of a piece, rather than just a particular surface color.

Opposite: Notable antiques dealer and appraiser, Charles Flint of Lenox, Massachusetts, owns this rare two-toned cupboard. He makes the best use of its primitive sensibility by surrounding it with his collections – including a handmade farm shovel and bottles, some of which are primitive.

This is a refurbished old primitive dry sink with doors removed in order to make a convenient storage and display area.

The new, small apothecary on the kitchen counter was painted to emulate the blue single door cupboard.

Although each of these three pieces of primitive furniture is different from the others, their taupe color makes a unified design statement. This is an elegant corner in a historic Bucks County Pennsylvania home.

This two-tone cupboard is as pretty inside as outside; for that reason, this homeowner chooses to leave it open most of the time.

Opposite: This salmon milk painted trunk makes the perfect storage unit; it is now being utilized by this homeowner pretty much for the same purpose for which it was designed and made.

This creatively designed corner carries primitives beyond the historic home and into high style. The small dresser, the early clock face, and the child's primitive bentwood chair are all nice pieces, but together in this arrangement they become a wow part of the room.

The color of the milk paint and the simplicity of the piece make this yet another favorite of its owner, a long time passionate primitives collector.

The built-in stove and dishwasher surrounded by milk painted blue actually look like one primitive piece furniture.

For collectors, other prized surfaces on primitives include signs of wear that reflect their actual use. Alligatoring, crackling, and fading of paint or stain show long use and are highly sought after. Wear in the obvious places — where clasps and wooden (or, sometimes, metal) fasteners are turned, handles and knobs are pulled, and shelves and tabletops are worn by decades or centuries of objects being placed on them — are welcome signs to the aficionado. Rat holes and old patched repairs are also collector favorites because these things show a history of the piece being used — adding those indefinables such as personality and character.

Also, because these pieces were passed from one generation to another, sometimes they were restored and repainted. Over time, bits of layers of earlier milk paint applications bleed through. This layered look is also prized by collectors.

A vintage table with a distressed finish is tricked out as a primitive. With white on white collections, it has the plain feeling of rural rustic style.

The tins are rusted and the surface somewhat the worse for wear on this old, handmade pie safe, but for some avid collectors, this sad condition adds to the charm of the piece.

Opposite: The shape and surface of this piece make it highly desirable among primitive collectors; talk about dramatic proportions.

This is ultimate primitive style

Opposite: This very primitive storage piece
works perfectly as a bathroom vanity.

Furniture doesn't come more rustic, but the worn surface of the pie safe seems to tell a story about its life and is certainly an attention-grabber. Beyond the surface, note the extensive workmanship on the base and crown.

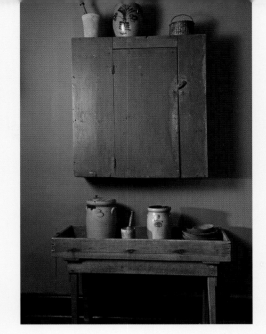

The sorting table topped by the petite storage cabinet created a great corner of this dining room for this northern Indiana family.

What they did

AS IN MOST FORMS OF ART AND craftsmanship, there are no hard and fast rules. Despite the simplicity of most primitive furniture, some makers copied, with surprising skill, the workmanship of finer country pieces or even those well-known makers and designers who created elegant furniture for people of more comfortable means. These homespun artisans sometimes included their version of a Queen Anne foot on a table, a Chippendale-style scroll, an imitation Hepplewhite tapering table leg,

The stark simplicity of this arrangement of this mounted slant top desk and the cabinet above is what draws people to things primitive; the inspired composition is what makes all of us linger in front of it.

or just a graduating set of drawers on a bureau because they saw it once or it just looked right. They would chamfer a door or dovetail a drawer just because it would look better. Unschooled, untrained, the workmanship still had that quality that separated those pieces into a genre all their own.

Michelangelo, the master artist and sculptor of the Renaissance, who lived 500 years ago and is still acknowledged as one of the greatest artists and craftsmen of all time, said that in each block of stone there was a figure hidden waiting to be revealed. The goal, Michelangelo explained, was to clear away everything unnecessary and to expose the figure within the stone. The best craftsmen and furniture makers, whether highly trained and schooled or self taught and naïve, also coax the form out from within the raw wood.. They work with the wood and get a sense of what they can do to bring out the piece. We have heard carpenters and cabinet makers say that the piece, itself, tells the woodworkers how to create it. That sensibility does not ask for credentials or certificates of education.

The piece that closes primitive cabinets is nothing more than a small block of wood that turns on a spike or long screw. The color and texture of the wood as well as the basic lines is what primitive is all about.

Primitives seem to tell a story. We don't need to know the specifics of the day-to-day lives of those who made and used them. We do know that their lives were all about survival. We have a sense of what precious little time they had for fun and relaxation; work was at the crux of each day. We can imagine what it was like to shake their calloused hands. When we let the furniture and other items they made speak to us, this is what we see and hear. This is why primitives speak so strongly to so many people.

Opposite: This Queen Ann style table was either a formally made table that fell on hard times or a primitive where the maker emulated a famous style.

Getting down to basics

SOME PRIMITIVE FURNITURE BEGS for aesthetic value. These pieces are raw, unrefined, ungraceful, and roughly joined. Still, they warrant a special kind of appreciation.

Not to be dismissed, these objects do have a sensory value. Although crude, they are, in fact, the genesis of all furniture and speak volumes about the conditions in which their builders lived. Their obvious age, the wear that comes from decades (if not centuries) of use, expresses their rustic heritage. Isn't that what collecting and living with primitive pieces is all about?

When asked how they define the word "primitive" when it comes to what they see in the pieces they so passionately collect, homeowner after homeowner, collector upon collector say that it is more a feeling than a specific dictionary definition. They say that primitive furniture is as much about the emotion that the piece conveys than what goes into the making or look of the object. It is this raw, basic quality that offers universal appeal.

The most basic primitives can be an acquired taste and there are any number of people who just don't get it. They are not for everyone but, to be fair, very few things are.

Opposite: As with many primitive chairs, this one is milk painted in a soft tone. Also frequently seen, the seat is painted to match the wood. Other similar chairs were either caned or rush covered.

This is another vision of time travel. Very few pieces of furniture could represent the epitome of an early rural home as much as this open pine cabinet. It is basic and butt-joined; the nails bled rust through to the wood and it is clearly very old.

Shelves built into a wall or storage areas create what was known as a buttery – a place to store items for the kitchen. It is essentially a pantry. This homeowner from Indiana used it to store her non-essential, but wonderful primitives.

Below: A primitive box tucked under a country bed gives the feeling of an all primitive bedroom.

Some of us who live with primitives — either as a complete lifestyle or just the occasional piece — start with those raw and rustic objects that have little embellishment or standard aesthetic values. Then, as time goes on and we absorb the nature of primitive furniture and develop a greater sense of the qualities that separate one piece from another, we move on. We want those pieces that show a greater ability in workmanship and skill — still within the borders of primitive — than the more rudimentary objects. But, from the most basic to the most creative, and everything in-between, we can enjoy and admire it all.

Today, the enjoyment, appreciation and understanding of primitive furniture have developed into a culture. It's not that we all want to return to those days of early American rural lifestyle, but we like absorbing some of that culture into our lives.

We can question the growing attraction of primitives and try to explain it. It's so much easier to analyze what is valuable about an early American Chippendale highboy, the craftsmanship involved in making a Victorian Belter style chair, or the elegance of an original Louis XIV settee. It is harder to articulate the beauty of a simple, well-proportioned bucket bench, dovetailed as well as butt-joined, with home-made nails and crazing over milk paint with a rat hole in a back board. It's not unlike trying to explain great improvisational jazz to a person who has heard only classical music.

The homeowners married the direct lines of this rustic looking green cabinet to the timber framing of their house creating a linear sensibility throughout.

The pottery collection is displayed in an open pine cupboard. The lines of the furniture are simple and linear, typical of the primitive style

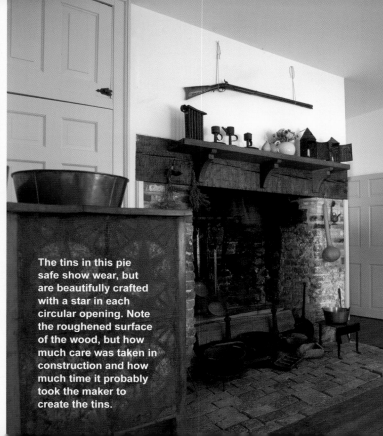

The tins in this pie safe show wear, but are beautifully crafted with a star in each circular opening. Note the roughened surface of the wood, but how much care was taken in construction and how much time it probably took the maker to create the tins.

The bathroom vanity designed to look like primitive furniture conveys an antique feeling to this new cabin.

The boldly patterned quilt adds a great backdrop for this little primitive chest.

This bowl rack – as well as the items in it – is simple and functional. It is the essence of primitive furniture, but the maker likely borrowed the whaleback design from a piece of more formal New England furniture.

Reproductions

AS WITH ANYTHING ELSE OF VALUE, there is a limited quantity of antique and vintage primitive furniture. Where there's a need, there's a market; and where there's a market, there are enterprising people who satisfy the demand.

People who love primitives — who enjoy the look, but don't necessarily care about an aged piece — are happy with newly made furniture designed in the style of early ones. The lines of new pieces, often made by skilled hobbyists, are close in style to antique and vintage pieces.

This newly decorated primitive offers a whimsical take on antique pieces.

Opposite: This is a well-made piece of new primitive furniture. It follows the clean lines and minimal crown molding of early cupboards.

A new hunt board made in the primitive style topped by a pine cupboard and collections of porcelain offer eclectic style.

This is a well-made piece of new primitive furniture. It follows the clean lines and minimal crown molding of early cupboards.

Opposite: A talented cabinet maker copied
a primitive style when making these new
kitchen cabinets.

An all new, primitively-styled cabinet, under a cleverly designed stand-up sink with a vintage water faucet, makes quite the dramatic statement in a somewhat small, entrance foyer bathroom.

Today's makers of primitives have varying skills at reproducing the surface of antiques, and can often match the joinery and the worn look of long-time use. As long as these pieces are sold as "new" or "reproduction," their presence is a real plus for those who love rustic furniture. In fact, many who buy these objects prefer the concept and the visual effect that reflects the early country lifestyle without the grunge of antiques. The newly made primitive has gained a strong position in the primitive buying marketplace.

In fact, there are some professional furniture makers specializing in creating antique-appearing primitives. They make no secret that the pieces are new. But their work is so fine that some of their pieces carry a greater market value than antiques.

Opposite: Hard as it is to believe, this salmon milk painted cupboard is a brand new piece created by skilled New England artisan, Jack Fisher.

Color and shape of new kitchen cabinets, both upper and lower, imitate primitive furniture in form and style. The variation in colors of each cabinet gives a sense of originality to the space.

Opposite: The small primitive chest blends perfectly with the arts and crafts period lamp with its simple lines and warm glow. It also marries perfectly with the log walls.

The two tone primitive cupboard adds an early touch to new and reproduction country style accessories. The Vermont homeowner placed it perfectly beneath those vertical logs.

This homeowner tried as much as possible to create the all-primitive home. The kitchen cabinets, although newly made, are done in an early primitive style and she surrounded them with primitive accessories to emphasize the feeling of the space

This primitive pine cupboard, with just a bit of molding that neatly finishes off the top, holds a collection of vintage and antique yellow ware bowls. There is also a vintage wheel of fortune, an early bowling pin and an antique quilt. It is the cupboard that unifies this disparate group of collectibles.

While a fake is, in fact, a reproduction, not all reproductions are fakes. A fake is made to fool the buyer into thinking that he or she is buying an antique. A reproduction, however, is made to look like the real deal to fit in with the look of their home and collections and does not pretend to be an antique.

The effort and sweat that originally went into the one-of-a-kind pieces are those elements that we can be reminded of when we look at or own a reproduction. However, the originality, the individual histories and survivability of the individual, original objects can't be reproduced; it is those things that drive the purists and the collectors.

Whether to purchase an antique or a reproduction is a personal, subjective decision and, while it is critical in the marketplace or to purists, this is not a pivotal issue in discussions about interior design.

This arts and crafts cabinet is not really primitive, but the stark, basic construction, simple lines and emphasis on the grain of the wood certainly suggest rusticity. It blends well with objects such as the real primitive bowl on the base shelf.

New make-do chairs are hot in the market place. Not always historically accurate, they offer the primitive collector a relatively comfortable place to sit.

The high-standing jack-booted kitchen cabinet, in simple off-white paint, is the perfect lead-in to the hallway. Its narrow dimensions make it an easy fit almost anwhere.

The small panes of glass in the cupboard look like the old windows in the earliest houses with the panes separated by multiple mullions. Also note how age and the environment have warped the dining room tabletop in front.

Well-worn primitive corner cupboard holds family treasures. Note the layers of paint put on over time. Some collectors think of this as grunge and avoid it; others love the look and feel it speaks to the lives and history of the piece.

This primitive postal mail holder mounted over a primitive desk repurposes both pieces as the corner can now function as a small office. The maker of the top piece clearly went to great effort to create a refined piece.

Another high style arrangement using primitives and other pieces – all of the same tone –creates a dramatic composition.

This cabinet is strictly vintage, but the piece and the rough surface give it a historic feeling.

This handmade bench creates the entire primitive feeling in this New England sun room.

The piece makes the collection. Solid, well made primitive farm tables with scrub tops are always in demand.

The homeowner wanted her home to have a totally primitive feeling. However, she gave a nod to comfort in her mix of furniture styles because the family needed someplace to sit. This was her solution to the issue of comfort versus authenticity. The sofa offers primitive in simplicity and borrows blue checked pattern on upholstered pieces from Early American simple. The bench, which is being used as a coffee table and the shelf above the couch are true early primitives.

This ultra plain primitive pie safe, when accessorized by blue and white dishes, creates a dressier space than if the blue trim of the windows and the porcelain pieces were not there. Furniture does not sit in a vacuum; its placement is dictated and affected by what surrounds it.

This homeowner has a great collection of all things primitive as well as somewhat more refined country pieces. The dining table and pewter cabinet are among her favorite pieces.

Opposite: A wonderful and petite bucket bench in early red fits perfectly against a yellow-mustard wall. For interest, depth, and mood, even with primitives, color is king.

Early primitive benches such as this one are difficult to find.

THERE ARE MYRIAD WAYS THAT people who love primitive furniture use it in their homes. Some, as shown in this chapter, go all out and totally embrace the rustic lifestyle. Theirs are the entirely primitive homes in which each piece is handpicked for antique accuracy. If it isn't vintage or antique, these homeowners just won't have it. There are also those who keep within the visual context of the all-primitive home, but do include the prerogative of well-made reproductions.

There is symmetry and balance in the placement of the furnishings in this very primitive room. The vertically boarded walls placed near the horizontal logs create a dynamic composition.

This is definitely a no bells and whistles kitchen – there is not a granite countertop or stainless appliance to be seen anywhere.

This aesthetic and philosophy goes well beyond the furniture. For these homeowners, a primitive house is as much about lifestyle as it is about décor. While most often a necessary nod is given to 21st century amenities (who really wants an outhouse as opposed to indoor facilities, a wood burning cook stove rather than gas or electric?), their home is a venue in which to live in a previous generation — a generation that speaks to them more than current times. This lifestyle emulates 19th century life in the countryside, on the plains and in the small towns of a more rugged, less opulent and pampered America. Beyond furnishings in these homes, there is an aura of early times. Lights are kept low, sometimes even fueled almost entirely by kerosene or candle. What 21st century amenities there are — and often there aren't many — are disguised; flat screen televisions are tucked into primitive cupboards; computers and other electronic conveniences are also hidden and camouflaged. It's not just about the look, it's about wanting to live more simply, the way people lived multi generations ago.

Opposite: With its finely made cabinetry, this kitchen is primitive in décor without necessarily looking historic. In the historic home, kitchen cabinets would most likely be individual pieces of cabinetry and not matching units – but this works and certainly is in keeping with the primitive aesthetic.

This rustic looking kitchen cabinetry goes far in creating an all primitive feeling.

This kitchen is both practical and of primitive style.

Here too, the main room is for cooking, eating, and spinning.

Typical of a true historic primitive house, the main room was not only used for the family to rest and relax, it was also the place of work. Here, the parlor also serves as a quilting room.

Room by room

NAMES OF ROOMS TAKE ON EARLY descriptions; the family refers to the living room as the parlor, keeping, or gathering room; pantries are butteries; these being the words used to describe those spaces in generations past.

In the kitchen, all evidence of modern appliances are hidden, camouflaged or modified to take on the appearance of a historic home. The refrigerator will be behind panels of wood; when not in use, the stove top is kept covered by a large breadboard and small appliances are otherwise tucked out of sight.

In the sitting room, allowances for comfort include, perhaps, an antique wing chair and fabric-covered furnishings made of wood and cushioned by pillows stuffed with feathers or down. Spring supported furnishings of the 20th and 21st century are rare.

This is the ultimate historic looking primitive kitchen. The furniture and the wood burning cook stove are authentic and imitate perfectly the rooms and lifestyle of the people who lived in 19th century rural America.

Elegant half-open shelving unit makes a great primitive design statement placed against the rustic, roughly textured stone wall.

Birch bark, sticks, and twigs create the primitive Adirondack style that is typical of upstate New York.

In the bedroom of this Cape Cod, Massachusetts, historic house, the beautifully made primitive pencil post bed is enhanced by the rustic bench at the foot and the rare red bed steps.

The dining room is probably furnished the closest to similar contemporary spaces. Here, we find early dining tables and chairs, with primitively designed china cupboards and hutches. In the all-primitive household, however, usually the only light comes from a chandelier and perhaps a candle or two sitting on the table.

Bedrooms often feature rope beds, with trundles below; not necessarily comfortable, but carrying forward the historic demeanor.

Sometimes, window treatments, if any, are nothing more than a square of burlap or linen attached to the corner of the window. This spare look goes well with the quiet attitude of the overall décor.

Kids didn't often have their own rooms in early cabins. They were lucky to get their own bed.

Not only is the furniture typical of the all primitive home, it's the absence of any decorative enhancement at all that typifies that style. There is no art or any other kind of adornment in the room.

Typical of most primitives, the standing, double-doored cupboard, the pencil post bed, round pine table, four-drawer dresser, and the hanging cupboard all are unadorned. In each case, their beauty is in the richness of the wood surface and the balanced proportions of their design.

You can't tell a
book by its cover

MANY OF THE INTERIORS OF THESE all-primitive homes have nothing at all to do with the exterior look or style. One of our favorite all-primitive homes was created in a mid-20th century Georgian-style structure. Another had a ranch house exterior, and a third was actually a doublewide partially standing on cinder block. There's one, with pictures included in this chapter, that was a recently built "McMansion" on a cul-de-sac in a contemporary sub-development. How impassioned primitive lovers design their interiors can have little or nothing to do with the structure of the house and the neighborhood in which it stands.

Historically, the windows in primitive homes were small — both because glass was expensive and in consideration of insulation (see the chapter on Architecture). Also, rooms weren't very large and many of them were multi-use. Today, however, even some of the all-primitive purists tend to have larger window expanses and, while what they call their rooms might be similar to those in the old days — keeping room, gathering room, etc. — often the sizes of these rooms are somewhat larger and brighter as natural light flows in through large windows or glass French doors leading out to patios.

The point being that these are lived-in homes and not museums and, while people do what they can to modify their environments to the lifestyle they prefer, in the end, their furnishings and amenities usually make some allowances for comfort and practicality.

A peek into an early and rustic home.

Opposite: This homeowner has gone as primitive in her décor as she possibly can. The look is pure rustic – yet utilizing clean, open space.

In as primitive a house as this one, homeowners were right in using benches as seating. It's not that chairs would not have been used, but the bench gives an authentic historic look. This is, in fact, a new house where the builder used reclaimed barn board for the walls.

This is a great example of a tall cupboard – also sometimes known as a chimney cupboard. This is because of their usual placement in front of chimneys. This piece, with its bright blue original paint, great lines, and honest wear, is a standout even in this all-primitives house and would make any collector happy.

This 19th century log cabin was moved from Kentucky to Indiana and probably looks the same way inside as when it was originally built.

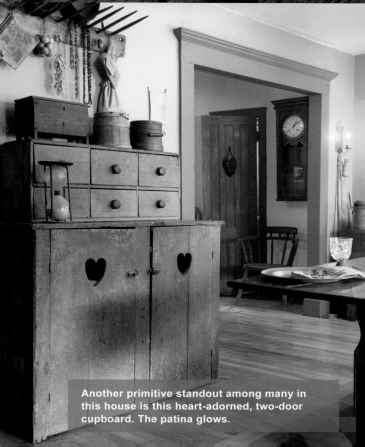

Another primitive standout among many in this house is this heart-adorned, two-door cupboard. The patina glows.

Stepping from one room into the next in this house, one would never know that a 21st century family lives there.

This is a typical multi-purpose gathering room.

This is an elegantly created, but still primitive daybed; it is simple and uncomfortable.

This little bedroom has a quiet antique elegance that, in part, is why so many are attracted to primitives.

Opposite: Simple, rustic, and basic, this bathroom
epitomizes the definition of primitive.

Opposite: Even though the elegant and formal American secretary in the foreground is vastly different in style from the gray, milk painted dining room cupboard in the adjoining dining room, by their size and shape they balance each other.

This is the New Mexican/Spanish version of primitive in a home in the outskirts of Santa Fe. Given the rustic, old world architecture with its exposed beams and simple furniture, the primitive bench adds the perfect touch of rural, rustic Americana.

THERE ARE THOSE WHO BLEND furniture styles in their homes, mixing Pilgrim with Federal, Country, Victorian, Deco, Loft/Industrial, and everything in-between. There is often some primitive furniture in that mix. They usually refer to their look as eclectic.

It's remarkable — only using their innate visual sensibility — how many homeowners, comfortably and effectively, join two or more styles. They do this without the resources of professional interior designers, but by using their own sense of what looks good. And, it works.

This rustic room combining an early milk painted trunk with a simple vintage sofa and an antique quilt and the all over design statement is country- primitive.

These Cape Cod homeowners have blended periods and styles with a contemporary, but simple, sofa juxtaposed to a primitive trunk serving as a coffee table, with a primitive open cupboard in the background. The folky, red-painted deer head sculpture on the wall acts as a binder to the two areas.

An antique primitive trunk centered in a set of vintage leather chairs is the linchpin for the rural look of the room.

Country — high, low, and across the seas

THE MIX MOST FREQUENTLY SEEN in country design is the combination of starkly primitive with more decorative country style furnishings and accessories. This blend of country and primitive is, of course, a natural; there is such a fine line separating the two that sometimes there is hardly a defining line at all.

All antique primitives are country, but all country antiques are not primitive. So, it is not surprising that people interchange country and primitive pieces, since the basic differences, beyond the telltale expertise of the makers and whether or not an object is handmade, lie in the adornments and carving that are more common in high country furnishings.

These houses often are not spare; many have abundant displays of antique and vintage collections that include stacked measures, dolls and other vintage toys, new and antique stuffed animals, decoys, baskets (hanging and piled), and other objects usually suggestive of rural life. Sometimes, walls are painted in bold tones and a stenciled border is applied just below the ceiling. The colors come from the Colonial and Federal periods when use of vibrant reds and blues on walls made brown furniture pop.

This room exhibits a great mix of country feeling styles, given the primitive trestle table and the more formal Windsor chairs. The metal horse weathervane is stark and effective, and gives a balance to the dining corner.

Opposite Top: A country-style floor cloth, Windsor chairs, and early American wainscoting are perfect dining room mates to the primitive table in this light, bright, and airy West Virginia dining room.

Opposite Bottom: In this room, but for the two Windsor chairs, it's all primitive. Windsors, although originally used, in part, as casual outdoor furniture, have over time taken on a more formal look.

The formal comb-back Windsor chair blends well with the adjacent blue hanging cupboard and the primitive table; this corner of a dining room offers a primitive design look.

This full look also includes quilts, coverlets and throw pillows on chairs and sofas. Early paintings, hand painted signage of rural commerce, and other hangings cover walls.

There are no hard and fast rules or definitive borders between the spare look of the purely primitive home and the fuller, vintage country look. Many houses are a little of both. Certainly, in the totally primitive home, there are still collections of objects of the period, while in a house furnished with the slightly more refined country furniture, there will still be primitive furnishings in the mix.

A Federal bedroom in Cape Cod, with its variations on blue, is enhanced by the simple lines and warm milk paint painted blanket chest at the foot of the bed. It is so appropriate, that without it, the room would seem stiff and formal.

The very early trestle table that has survived time and use, and, no doubt, many owners, completes this well decorated Federal period dining room.

An antique storage bench with great surface and desirable ball feet fits perfectly against a wall in this newly built log cabin that has an old-time flavor. More formal country pieces add to the rustic, rural atmosphere.

Somewhat more distant, the English- or French-style country home that so many Americans emulate offers a comfortable balance to American primitive furniture. The play on lines, textures, and color gives European country homes richness and interest. In these rooms, the meshing of styles creates a singular aesthetic. A primitive table tucked between two chintz-covered club chairs becomes a single unit with the pattern and colors of the fabric blending with the texture and surface of the simple wood table.

Sometimes, all it takes is one good primitive (see the table between the two easy chairs) to offer a primitive feeling to a space. This is a rustic corner of a Dallas, Texas, kitchen.

A sitting area that would be fashionable in any era is made that much more informal and comfortable with the inclusion of the primitive table tucked between two more formal chairs. That one piece of rustic furniture adds texture and charm.

This old primitive country store counter top works beautifully as a small kitchen island, but also blends well with the more contemporary white cabinets.

Everything old is new again

For years, primitive furniture and style remained largely among those whose heart is in the country décor. Today, use of primitives is expanding and evolving. It's not just the spare style of primitives themselves that creates their special look, it's also the unadorned feeling of the rooms in which they exist. Those who live in wildly popular city loft and rehabbed factory living spaces with high ceilings, floor to ceiling windows and barely disguised industrial duct work have also embraced primitive furniture. The stark simplicity of the lines and the plain finishes make a dramatic fit with the rough hewn look of these housing units.

This is especially true for younger people who have a prejudices view of antiques as the giant, old, palm-filled Asian urns guarding their grandmother's front hall, or who are just turned off by what they consider overwrought, "fussy" antiques with doodads and filigrees.

Minimalists who wouldn't touch anything carved Victorian or gilded European are now clamoring for primitive antiques and folk art to highlight their modern living spaces. This widening circle of interest is one of the major reasons that the primitives market has been soaring in recent years; it's no wonder that dealers and shop owners specializing in primitives are smiling. Their only problem lately is replacing the one-of-a-kind items that are flying out their doors.

There is sound reasoning for this. Any design primer will say that in good decorating there are at least two major objectives: the objects in a room should blend well; they should advance an overall look. There should also be a central focal piece to create a counterpoint — an accent piece — to avoid a sense of sameness and a stagnant quality to the space. This, in

The primitive blue cabinet, coupled with the contemporary painting, in this new Nantucket, Massachusetts, timber frame home provides dramatic high style.

A rustic workman's bed, refurbished to hold a glass top, works as a coffee table in this modernized, but historic, home in northeastern New York. The primitive qualities of the architecture, including the wood and exposed beamed ceiling and the wide plank pine floors, blend beautifully with the mid-century modern furniture and the primitive pieces. This is the perfect example of primitive melding with contemporary.

other terms, is much the same way that salt or lemon heightens the taste of good food.

Utilizing primitives in a contemporary setting makes a win-win design statement and accomplishes both of the above goals. Architecturally, as well as in furnishings, the contemporary look is typified by simple lines, clean spaces, and minimal adornment. The inclusion of primitive furniture and art, with their simplicity of design and placement, in a contemporary setting advances that style. At the same time, with their aged appearance, they also provide a great contrast to modern furnishings and new architecture.

In working to the limits of design theory, the mix of primitive artwork and furniture with highly contemporary furnishings produces a visual home run. This is especially true of primitive-style folk art where decorative objects transcend their function. Hang a large, bold Amish quilt, with its geometric shapes and deeply colored patterns,

on the wall of a clean-lined, streamlined contemporary room and suddenly the quilt looks like modern art. The same could be said of an antique, homemade checkerboard, carnival wheel of fortune, or merchant's hand printed sign.

This also works with mixing furniture styles. Take a modern sofa and place a primitive table or bench in front of it to be used as a coffee table and the look remains modern. The table will highlight and point up the lines of the sofa more effectively than a contemporary table and at the same time, its age and patina will play against the newness of the surrounding furnishings.

The glass topped primitive workman's stand serves as a side table to a contemporary sofa. Juxtaposed to an early structural post, it defines a simple, clean sensibility that occurs when primitives are used with other periods and styles of furniture.

It is not just the similarities between primitives and contemporary pieces that make their blend work so well. The beauty in their relationship is also in their contrasts. These include huge differences in the surfaces of modern and antique pieces. Old wood, painted or untouched, will have a quality of richness and depth rarely seen in newly constructed pieces. Patina, the rich surface modification that comes from wear, use, and age, typically defines much of the antique quality of a piece. Copper and bronze turn an elegant, soft green as they age. Painted and natural wood surfaces soften over time and their surfaces show graceful wear. Even with their simple lines, primitives convey timelessness. The textural differences, juxtaposed to — and dovetailed into — each other, create an almost physical experience that adds a subtle strength to a space.

The owner of this nineteenth century renovated tobacco barn, converted into a private residence, used a mix of primitive and more traditional country pieces in her historic home. The focal point of the room is the large primitive harvest/dining table. Although she has surrounded her table with finely made country chairs, this homeowner has pushed the design envelope even further by including modern art in her contemporarily re-designed space.

Rustic, uncomfortable simplicity in this early American room that is anything but welcoming is emphasized by the direct and unadorned lines of the corner primitive hutch. This piece neatly pulls both sides of the room together.

And the beat goes on...

TODAY, PRIMITIVE FURNISHINGS are also used in combination with other more divergent styles. The simplicity of primitive furniture can provide contrast to the formality of Federal, but works within that early genre as the two fall within similar historic periods.

On the surface, there is little similarity between primitive and mid-century modern furniture and the high style linear quality of Art Deco. But there is compatibility in their respective simple lines that primitives can emphasize, which makes either of the two modernistic styles a good blend with rustic furnishings.

There is no road map to primitive design, but there can be a bit of an explanatory or analytical path through the maze of styles. As in all kinds of home design, each house is unique and different, presenting the individual stamp of the people who live in them.

In this dining room, a mix of George Nakashima chairs, vintage art pottery vases, and the simple primitive gray cupboard blend perfectly and boldly.

A refurbished primitive cabinet, now holding a sink, sits under an Eastlake Victorian mirror and is surrounded by a wall of incidentals and accessories. Primitives are not only at home in this fascinating rural Pennsylvania bathroom, but create the overall atmosphere.

Just one simple primitive hanging cupboard gives an early, rustic feeling to the entire area, even though the adjacent blue primitive-style cupboard is new and the chair, although imitative of historic furniture, is not primitive at all.

The primitive style coffee table, actually a cut down farmer table, pulls the entire room together. It is large and occupies center stage in this new log home.

The secretary is a great example of a beautifully made primitive. The maker created it in the style of fine furniture. It is adjacent to two Connecticut-made chairs and a primitive table. All four pieces blend well in this Kentucky living room.

A series of primitive items – document box, wall sconce, hanging cabinet and other objects – create an intriguing corner on a second floor stair landing.

Opposite: This hand made banjo, probably fashioned from the top of a measure or primitive box, rests in a rustic chair waiting for its player to strum some old country tunes. Homemade – rather than store bought – musical instruments were more likely to be found in farmsteads. This one is a primitive gem.

CHAPTER IV:

ACCENTS & ACCESSORIES:

ICONS OF RURAL LIFE

An early handmade, but worn, metal pitcher full of wild flowers tucked into a bookshelf says rustic country.

A contemporary primitive peg board as a towel rack placed above a rustic open cupboard used for towel storage offers the solution to no closet in the bathroom.

Left: Series of country and primitive crocks and fragments make super design elements in this kitchen.

All of the small pieces in this arrangement, with the exception of the lamp, are handmade and unschooled. The wood decoy was a real find for this avid collector.

ART, ACCESSORIES, AND ACCENTS are what advance and complete the look of any room, especially those that are primitive in style. Whether or not your entire house is in the primitive style, it's just in a single room, or you mix up your otherwise non-primitive interior with the occasional rustic piece of furniture, accents enhance the primitive feeling.

The purely primitive decorator would limit art and other accents to the kinds of things that early, rural families would have used, such as portraits or paintings, samplers, and perhaps maps. However, most people, even the most ardent primitive fans, expand their artwork and accessories, opting not to practice rigid adherence to a primitive lifestyle.

The blue primitive box is both practical for storage and adds a pop of design impact because of its large size.

This illustrates how each strong piece, when grouped with others, creates an even bolder design statement. Each of the three elements in this image is an unadorned antique primitive. The bowl is burl, hand carved from a knot in a tree. The nineteenth century hanging cupboard was made by hand planing pine boards. The small trunk was probably a simple family document box. Each of them is bold in its simplicity. Juxtaposed in one design vignette, the three pieces, as an arrangement, advance the look of the entire room. No line is wasted; the décor adds up to uncluttered, clean elegance.

Except for the primitive design accents that include a handmade log cabin model, a sampler, and a hand carved rooster gathered on the dresser at right, most of the furnishings are more high country than primitive. Put together, the room is made less formal and more rustic.

The current generation has come to appreciate the beauty, workmanship and artistry of all kinds of objects never originally intended as decorative. We now see them as works of art and feel free to use them as design pieces. They are reflective of the lifestyle of the era in which they were made, so we allow ourselves the liberty to make them part of our home design.

A mix of primitive and country accessories and artwork pulls together two quiet corners of the same Cape Cod, Massachusetts, living room.

Between the exposed beams that add a rustic architectural feeling and the hanging cupboard and other accessories, this corner of an Ohio suburban home could have been part of a 19th century primitive homestead.

These primitive kitchen elements create an authentic looking pantry nook.

Opposite: Two primitive boxes and a primitively – albeit contemporary – hand carved duck tucked into a window are proof that small details can make an effective statement.

The décor of this space is all about the primitive farming tools used as design accessories.

Therefore, even those with major collections of fine primitive furniture also incorporate such items as weather vanes and whirligigs, architectural remnants like corbels and finials, farm implements, and advertising signs. The rural household of another time would no more have had these things inside as part of their household than they would have brought livestock into their parlors.

Opposite: This homeowner used two primitives to create an effective vignette. The blue two-door cupboard is accessorized by her goat wagon. Normally an exterior piece, in this house it is used as a design accessory.

White-painted primitive farm tools creatively joined together make a huge and impactful statement. This is a great wow factor created at minimal cost.

The little white primitive table placed in the center of the seating arrangement, plus the arched window with a rough surface give a rustic appearance and anchor the primitive design feeling of the room

Design savvy people are blending primitive Americana with other styles. They are using color and textiles to establish that eclectic look. Here, the homeowners have taken a cleaned-lined modern sofa, covered it with classic primitive blue and white plaid cotton, and juxtaposed it to folk art and primitive furnishings. The look is clean, bold, and fresh. Most of all, the room remains appealing to those who love contemporary style because the simplicity of the space has not been compromised.

This late 18th century Pennsylvania farmhouse sets the perfect stage for utilizing a mix of traditional country pieces and primitives. Typical of old houses, this room has particularly deeply set windows into which the owner has displayed one of his primitive folk art whirligigs (primitively designed, whimsical wind toys).
Although the box in front of the sofa, used here as a coffee table, is rudimentary in its design and construction, the one adjacent to the fireplace is a more traditional, well-made country piece. It is grain painted – a faux or imitation of wood grain design popular in the mid- to late nineteenth century and frequently used in the creation of more formal country pieces. Note also the design use of the three horse weathervanes hung above the mantle. They are finely created copper pieces of strong traditional country design. The mix of the two styles works perfectly in this room; each enhances the other.

The ties that bind the primitive feeling in this Maryland home are the table in the midst of the seating arrangement and the rustic looking, arched white window frame.

In the dining room, a very rustic box, painted white to blend with the rest of the room, is elegant and deformalizes the room.

Antique and reproduction commercial signs, as well as vintage and antique game boards have become hugely popular accessories in rustic-style homes.

Everything in this space is new or vintage with a nod to primitive in the simplicity of the lines of the table. It is the five early primitive baskets on the rustic shelf that add a feeling of authenticity to the space.

The primitive, homemade weathervane rooster sets off a series of boxes and country collectibles and is a distinctive decorative element among these other objects.

In good primitive design one will also find collections of items that were made for specific functions. These include dolls and other toys, boxes and small cabinets with drawers, crocks, plates, pewter, and pottery. All might well have had a place in the early primitive home, but more often they were for function rather than design.

Other elements used in primitive room design are antique or vintage-style small objects that could even have been manufactured, but because of their age and design enhance the primitive look. As one example, kitchen utensils with colored handles are often seen tacked to walls and stuffed into crocks. They give an old-time feeling of rustic Americana to the room, without necessarily being authentic, individually made, hand done primitives.

Red- and green-handled kitchen tools are probably more vintage than antique, and they may not even be handmade, but when hanged on the handmade primitive rake with the log wall as a background and the overall effect is rural and rustic.

Rustic food preparation items add to the primitive décor of this kitchen.

Nineteenth and 20th century Halloween collectibles are hot ticket items. They are still being hand made for display.

This grouping of primitive accessories is particularly well put together because there is a similarity in color and tone that gives cohesiveness to the bathroom decor.

Common denominators

THEN THERE ARE THE IMPORTS. Every nation on every continent has a rural population that made and/or makes rustic furniture and accessories. Even the most experienced collector can have difficulty differentiating between rustic pieces made outside the U.S. with those made in Canada, Western and Eastern Europe, the Philippines, China, and other areas around the globe. There is no reason not to include them in one's design.

However, it's one thing not to know or even care about the original nationality of a piece; it's quite another when deception is involved. To further confuse the issue, not only are we dealing with the influx of Asian knockoffs in fashion and other areas, but there are also importers of items such as Chinese grain baskets that

are engraving American-style names on those pieces to give the impression that they are rural American antiques.

As in reproduction furniture, our only concern here is that if a piece is meant to deceive, then we all bridle at that marketing ploy and none us wants to be fooled. If it is clear what the piece is, without the motive of deception, then that's another thing.

Having said that, unless we are absolute and purist for only things American, incorporating pieces from other cultures, so that they fit in with the rustic tenor of an interior design, is appropriate. Beautifully made artifacts, regardless of their history or place of origin, can and should be respected for what they are and can certainly be included in one's décor. Rural peoples, regardless of their nationalities, all made primitive items for the same purposes. It's remarkable, when you view these objects from around the world, how similar many of them are in workmanship and style — defining the universal nature of their lifestyle and priorities.

Five small primitive objects in this kitchen corner produce a great rustic feeling. The top piece is a Chinese import, one of millions now flooding the American country primitive marketplace. They work well as primitive design pieces, as long as antique dealers sell them as imports and not American made. This rice measure was faked to be an American primitive with the English word, "Dairy" recently engraved on the side.

The pear painting was newly created in primitive style. With the addition of the early handmade rustic appearing pewter, the basket, and ironwork, they all work beautifully on a side table of an Indiana living room.

New markets and marketers

TODAY, THERE IS A RESURGENCE of crafters making homemade primitive-style pieces. Thousands of men and women have either seen the growing national trend to own handmade rustic items, or have gone beyond their hobbies of making such items just for themselves, their friends, and families, and decided to create home businesses in designing, making, marketing, and selling a variety of decorative, primitive-style objects.

Throughout the country, small businesses are starting up and flourishing whose owners are making a huge range of primitive accessories. These include candles, hooked-rugs, dolls, stuffed animals, signs, wreaths, flower boxes, candleholders, samplers, and every other imaginable item that has a primitive and rural sensibility.

This sitting room is given its rustic feeling by two small accents, the newly made primitive rug hung over the fireplace and the bench being used as a coffee table in front of the sofa.

Although many of these items are sold in shops, growing numbers of websites are also springing up, marketing homemade decorative accessories objects. These objects, individually designed and produced, demonstrate the talent and creativity of their makers, much like the original, vintage and antique primitives had a one-of-a-kind personality that defined each piece.

Primitive oil portrait on board of children gives an instant shot of rural rusticity to this relatively new kitchen.

The homeowner-made, primitively styled fireplace screen and the little footstool are effectively blended in combination with vintage country pieces in this Cape Cod, Massachusetts living room.

This grouping of primitive accessories, in similar tones of blue, provides a practical solution to storage needs and has strong visual appeal. Many of these objects are newly made for decorative purposes.

Mixed with rustic looking crocks, these two newly created primitive portraits lend just the right note to the dining room in a rural Virginia farmhouse.

The internet has given a voice and a presence to all these innovative and entrepreneurial people who can now market their homemade wares well beyond their doorsteps. At the same time, the homeowner who wants to find just the right piece to place on her candle stand or rustic mantle need go no further than her computer to complete that corner of her home.

That these objects are contemporary might dissuade some who want only antiques — but, these new objects offer the feel of the early primitive and, thus, have found a niche with a great many who are happy to create and live with — the look, feel and style of rustic Americana, whether it's just with the small primitive accessory or the entire house.

Despite the beautifully made new primitive cabinets, this southern California homeowner accessorized her kitchen with contemporary high-style, country-themed tiles. Although this may be a bit over the top for a primitive kitchen, the tiles do pack a visual wallop.

With its worn surface, this vintage cupboard gives all of the collectibles a rustic feeling.

Opposite: The old door, with original blue paint and blacksmith made hinges, adds a rustic backdrop to the homeowner-created concrete pot with dried wildflowers. This northern Indiana household has many such picturesque corners and details.

CHAPTER V:
ARCHITECTURE:
THE PRIMITIVE ENVIRONMENT

The handmade-styled brick walls and floor and rustic kitchen island say this is a primitive, farmhouse kitchen.

ALTHOUGH YOU CAN HAVE GREAT primitive-looking rooms in a tract house, it almost goes without saying that rooms full of fabulous rustic furnishings and accessories are enhanced by the architecture and design of the houses in which they are placed. Structural elements such as walls and floors not only blend with and emphasize rustic furnishings, but they also enrich the interior spaces.

Walls made of natural or roughened materials such as log, barn board, rough plaster, brick, and stone, suggest a historically primitive feeling in the architectural setting of any house. Exposed ceiling beams and wood floors with especially wide planks not only frame the interior design and its furnishings, but also add a textural tone and create a dimension of interest and mood.

Old posts and beams, with all the splits, scratches, and other imperfections that time and nature visited upon them, create an enveloping atmosphere of comfort and survival.

Although the French doors are contemporary, the table is high-style country and the fireside bellows are elegant folk art. The rustic posts and beams, dramatically framing the interior room and porch, lend a primitive aura to the space.

However, two other concepts also work. If one prefers more contemporary or formal furnishings and accessories, but still appreciates the rustic nature of structural materials, then an effective visual would be to surround an interior room with those materials that suggest a primitive, back-to-basics sensibility; this is a good way to have the best of both worlds.

The other concept, which is discussed more in the chapter on "Mixing It Up," is to enjoy primitive furnishings in architecturally designed spaces that are anything but primitive.

Minimalist cool

The real tie that binds primitives to contemporary is the notion that less is more. From an architectural view, a contemporary room will typically have windows with solid panes of glass and minimal trim instead of multiples of mullions. There will also be a sparseness of trim around doors, which are likely to be flat, instead of paneled; baseboards will be clean and simple, and trim between the ceiling and walls will be unobtrusive, if it is there at all. Furnishings and accessories, including art, will follow suit, both in paucity of pieces and the linear quality of their outline.

However, beyond the spatial and graphic similarities between primitive and ultra-contemporary, primitives add soul to contemporary rooms. New materials and modern design trends tend to convey a cool feeling. But, spare and modern do not, in fact, need to equate with cold. Primitives, with their aged patina and texture, offer these spaces inviting warmth that make them approachable and comfortable while keeping the modern motif consistent. By joining bold, contemporary furnishings and art in the same space as unpretentious primitives, a room crosses the single level of sameness into a vibrant, multi-layered living space.

Framing an open, bright area with weathered barn board adds a dimension and texture to the simplest and least cluttered interior design.

The utter starkness of this second-floor space, bordered by butt-joined posts and beams give the space a primitive emphasis.

Nothing is primitive about the furniture in this Chesapeake Bay home. However, given the old barn board surround, it becomes a fabulously primitive space that is clean and open and speaks of rusticity and informality.

Rustic beams, posts, and log walls add a primitive environment in this rural Virginia farmhouse.

Warming it up

In those areas where homeowners want the sense of structural and architectural elements to marry with their primitive furnishings, sometimes a little bit can go a long way — or one can even go the distance.

For example, stone and early brick hearths, fireplaces, and rough-hewn mantles and fireplace surrounds add a real feeling of history to almost any house of any age. Also, moldings and trims are minimal in the best primitive homes, but those that do exist are often butt joined and have little to no carving or adornments.

New windows, made in an old style, add a feeling of historic authenticity to the original log walls of this primitive bedroom.

This pass-through between old and new parts of a Virginia homestead, is pure rustic architecture.

The glass chandelier in this primitive Adirondack hallway tells us the homeowner has a sense of design whimsy.

The newly manufactured log walls, with their huge dovetails, help create a rustic feeling to the vintage items on the wall.

This old Vermont great room is made to feel primitive with walls of early red barn boards and rough cross beams.

The early door and the old, original paneling provide the authentic background for this primitive Buck's County, Pennsylvania bedroom.

One of the best things to happen to lovers of early homes is the advent of the architectural salvage store. If the room — or even the entire house — you want to appear rustic is more 1965 suburban than 1865 rural, antique and vintage doors and windows, usually plentiful in these venues, make super replacements for the hollow, bland-personality materials of new construction. Today, there are even window manufacturers who produce early looking, multi-paned glass with bubbles and waves that replicate age.

In most instances, keeping it simple will provide the best backdrop for primitive furnishings. However, there are no rules and, as shown in these pages, by looking at what homeowners around the country have effectively accomplished, the best design and marriage of architectural elements with interior furnishings and design is the one that works for you. Through these pictures, they can give you ideas, but they don't have your stuff or live in your home.

The rustic, newly made door fits in perfectly with the old log in this early cabin.

Working it your way

Regardless of when the house was built — or in what style — the interior can be created to be of whatever world you choose; there are no restrictions. When opting for a rustic feeling, however, it's most often best to keep your eye on the prize and decide what you are really trying to say about your living space.

Opposite: New, make-do, unskilled door trims only add to the rustic, primitive nature of this back porch – kitchen area. One of the benefits of a primitive environment is that one doesn't have to be a master carpenter to do home repairs and improvements that fit right in.

Typical of doors of the past, this double door kept out weather and uninvited visitors in the early days.

Opposite: A simple, uncluttered statement is made by this fabulously textured, homemade chair placed in front of a blue painted, board and batten-sided shed. Its serenity is inviting.

1849-BACK CREEK CABIN-1997

CHAPTER VI:

EXTERIOR SPACES &

OUTDOOR ROOMS

LANDSCAPERS AND GARDENERS refer to designed exterior areas as "outdoor rooms." These areas are considered part of our living space because our entire home, inside and out, is an integral part of our environment and lifestyle.

Porches, sheds and gardens are the perfect venues for outdoor primitive objects. Weathered by age and the elements, they add a wonderfully textured ambience to our entire homes.

These kinds of buildings — or parts of buildings — offer a real bonus to the entire property and, when enhanced by primitive objects, create a rustic, handmade quality to the home. Creatively placing primitive furnishings (made for the outdoors or not) along with handmade accessories and accent pieces not only offers appealing focal points to exterior areas, but can make use of those charming pieces that otherwise would be stored in that very shed (or basement or attic).

The following are various homeowners' ideas on how to further extend interior ambiance to the outdoors. In creating these spaces, they have added zing and beauty to their outdoor areas utilizing primitives they had on hand or couldn't resist buying, or they have just taken advantage of outdoor structures that had an enticing primitive feeling. Each season offers its own special treatment to these outdoor rooms and features; the richness and color of spring and summer, the full and vivid tones of autumn and the stark backdrop of winter.

Board and batten siding, through its vertical design, gives height and strength to any grouping. This arrangement of mixed materials – metal, wood, pottery and plants – is an effective vignette.

Opposite: The primitive artifacts on the exterior of a shed appear to be casually arranged, yet have a strong composition

This small, historic log cabin was moved from one spot in central North Carolina and rebuilt a few miles away. In this way, the cabin, which is the epitome of primitive, has been preserved.

Nothing could be simpler as a design statement than primitive, inexpensive jugs on a weathered pine board on a pond side property in North Carolina.

This porch on Cape Cod, open and inviting, tells visitors that they are entering the home of people who love rustic furnishings and original surfaces.

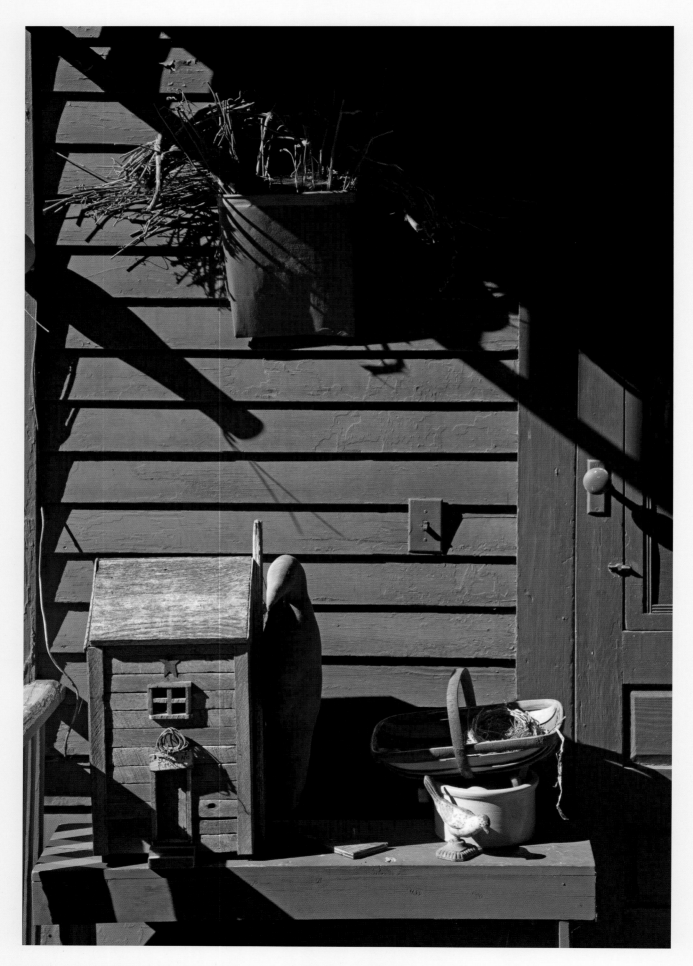

Light and shadow add a striking effect to this wonderful grouping of objects. The placement of those items, with their colors and textures, was not an accident.

The distressed wooden garden gate and homemade pergola create an inviting entranceway.

A porch post that was a toss-away makes a great stand for a birdhouse. Make-do's
are part of the essence of primitive furnishings in homes or gardens.

Washtub as flower box is the unique idea of American furnishings visionary and artist, Bob Timberlake, who created this use for an old graniteware tub. He also designed the innovative support using natural material.

Simple and dramatic composition works well in any season.

Winter brings its own visual aura to an exterior view that would be completely different in warmer weather.

Opposite: Seasonal decorations can be placed anywhere.

161

This homeowner in rural Virginia took advantage of the overall dimensions and placement and number of cross bars of a gate to a primitive shed to paint a naïve and folky version of an iconic symbol.

This autumnal display carefully composed on a back porch adds color and fun to an otherwise barren and uninteresting area.

Opposite: Old rusted tools, a beat-up chair, and a carpenter's box won't be diminished in value one bit – but add a charming corner to an outside, backyard area that suffers from being devoid of any interest.

One of the simplest, and yet most effective, tricks of display is to have multiple of the same kinds of objects grouped together. In this instance, the variety of watering cans adds a great look to this rural Kentucky home's back porch.

The simple primitive table with just two items on it gives a central focus to this Mississippi dog trot's covered walkway.

Opposite Top: Odds and ends and objects that would otherwise be piled in a shed are put to use to add interest and fun to a garden fence.

Small garden corners, if done well, are boosted by utilizing primitive and rustic items.

Opposite Bottom: An exterior, otherwise somewhat formal with its stained glass and lion fountain, is also an appropriate place to mix styles with a primitive table that is also functional.

Can you imagine this Ohio homeowner's delight when she found a good place for that old child's school desk she just couldn't resist? And, to top it off, it even has places to put those contemporary primitives?

We can hear them now, "Finally, we found a place to put all those bird houses that were just lying around."

This backyard patio area attached to a large, quite formal home in Greenville, Mississippi, is an ideal place to mix rustic objects where they blend together in look and function.

HOMEOWNERS

The authors wish to apologize for any possible omissions or other errors in this listing.